TRAIL

HER

TRASH

TRAIL
HER
TRASH

POEMS BY
LOLA NATION

EMP
Toledo, Ohio
http://www.empbooks.com

Copyright © 2018 Lola Nation

We find discussions of our rights - as publishers and authors - to be laughable, all things considered. Please claim this work as your own. Please republish it and sell it on street corners. Please include our material in ALL of your get-rich-quick schemes. All we ask is that you accept responsibility for any libel lawsuits. Speaking of which ... This book is a complete work of fiction. Names, characters, places, opinions, dreams, dates, impressions, monologues about a certain New York City basketball team, emotional trauma, statistics, and predictions are products of the author's imagination and/or are symptoms of mental illness. We are not in the business of accepting responsibility for anything and will deny we actually made this book and blame Jeff Hornacek at every turn.

First Edition

ISBN: 978-0-9997138-1-5
LOC: 2018938596

10 19 33 34 6 11 1973

Design, Layout, and Edits: Ezhno Martín
Cover Design: Jeanette Powers
Interior Photos: Lola Nation

T.O.C

POETRY AFTER MIDNIGHT.....1
STARBUCK'S ON 39TH.....2
YOU, ME AND THE THIRD DEGREE BURNS.....4
THE ACADEMY.....6
CRAMMED INN HEROIN TALES.....9
RACES.....10
UNLIKELY HEROS AMONG UNSUAL SUSPECTS.....12
ONE OF US (SPEED FREAK AND JUNKIES).....13
GLASS PIPES.....18
I WANT TO BE MORE CRYPTIC.....20
WHEN.....22
BEATBACK COVER.....24
IF WE ONLY HAD GROUPIES WE'D BE SET.....25
DIRECTIONS TO REVOLUTION BOULEVARD.....27
TIJUANA TAXI.....28
LIVING AFTER WE DIE.....31
TIJUANA GENERAL (A CASE OF STAPH, MRSA, A STROKE AND A COMA, PLACE YOUR BETS).....32
STRIDULATION.....38
OMERTA.....39
PART TWENTY-TWO LA RECHERCHE DU TEMPS PERDU.....41
BABY-DADDY COMES TO MISSOURI.....44
CHILDREN'S COURT (MONTEREY PARK, CALIFORNIA).....47
(THE FOSTER) DAUGHTER.....48
SAMANTHA MARIE.....49
SAMMIE, THE FIRST ONSET OF A MEMORY.....52
MR. DUMPTY'S APOLOGY IS REFUSED.....54
WHEN TAXI DRIVER MEETS FALLING DOWN.....55
TRANSLATION, GOD LISTENS: BITTER.....58
POETRY IS FOR MENTAL CASES, LOVEBIRDS AND THE DEAD.....60
AMUSEMENT PARK.....61
DUST DEVILS.....62
FUGUE.....63
TO DO LIST.....64

ENCOUNTERS.....66
BIBLICAL APPROACH.....70
GOOD YEAR.....71
PORTAMENTI.....73
CONSOLATION DOUBLE.....74
PERTAINYMS.....75
TAXING THE TARMAC.....77
COME HERE, WHAT DID YOU SAY?.....78
THE BEST REVENGE ON A LIAR IS TO CONVINCE THEM YOU BELIEVE.....79
GUILT RIDDEN (BET ON THAT HORSE). ENCORE AT HOLLYWOOD PARK. (EXACTA BOX).....81
EMERGENCE. SEE. (WHAT YOU MADE ME DO BEHAVIOR).....82
MUTATIONS.....83
LACK LUST HERE.....84
FRAGMENTS.....88
SOMEI YOSHINO - MONO NO AWARE....90
ARS LONGA, VITA BREVIS....91
TRAIL HER TRASH....93

IN PART FOR:

**SAMANTHA MARIE,
ERIN MIRAMONTES,
DANIEL PATCH**

POETRY AFTER MIDNIGHT

BRAWNY BARITONE,
HE READS HIS POETRY
SNEAKS UP THE COLUMNS
AND OPENS THE SKYLIGHT
AND I AM ALL STARRY-EYED
LYING ON MY BACK
FOR A PANORAMIC VIEW.

NAVY NIGHT, OCEANS WIDE
YOU ARE THE TIDE
AND I AM EVERY GRAIN OF SAND
UNEARTHED IN THE FRENZY
OF YOUR FORCE,
MESMERIZED.

STARBUCK'S ON 39TH

THE TABLE BY THE ENTRANCE
KEEPS THE CONVERSATION CLOSE TO THE DOOR,
HE HASN'T SEEN HER SINCE HE'S NOT SURE JUST WHEN,
SOMETIME BETWEEN THE LAST KISS
AND THE LAST OF HER FURNITURE HE CARRIED TO HER CAR.
SHE CUT HER HAIR, AS THEY ALWAYS DO,
SHE IS MAKING SMALL TALK
ABOUT COUPLES WHO ARE STILL TOGETHER, DID HE MEET THEM?
DOES HE REMEMBER?
SHE CONFESSES SHE SOLD HIS ART AT AN AUCTION
TO HIS SILENT DISMAY,
HE NO LONGER HANGS LARGELY IN HER LIVING ROOM,
SHE NOW RESIDES IN
STARK WHITE WALLS
BECAUSE SHE CAN'T BEAR TO DECORATE,
NOT YET.
HE SIPS BLACK COFFEE,
WHILE SHE STIR-STICKS HER PAPER CUP
SMILING NERVOUSLY, TALKING INCESSANTLY TO FILL
THE EMPTY SPACE THAT USE TO BE CONSIDERED
ONE
TRUE
LOVE.

THE TABLE BY THE SOON TO BE INCONVENIENT SOUND
OF THE COFFEE GRINDER HAS AN NERVOUS MAN,
LOOKING AT EACH WOMAN WHO PASSES THROUGH THE DOOR,
THINKING, *YES, HE COULD*,
THEN SHE FINALLY ARRIVES,
SHE ZEROS IN,

WALKS RIGHT UP TO THE EMPTY CHAIR,
DROPPING HER MAGENTA COAT, REVEALING A HOT PINK SWEATER
AND PLAID ANKLE LENGTH SKIRT
IN MATCHING STITCHES OF OFF THE RACK COLOR.
SHE IS TWENTY TO THIRTY POUNDS MORE
THAN HE IMAGINED FROM THE DATED PICTURES HE'D RECEIVED.
THEY DISCUSS WORK, ALCOHOL, AND SNIPERS.
THEIR VOICES ABOVE THEIR REGULAR OCTAVES,
SPEAKING FASTER THAN VERBALLY COMFORTABLE,
HURRYING RIGHT ALONG,
PAUSING ONLY BETWEEN CHRISTMAS BLENDS
BAGGED FOR REGULAR CUSTOMERS
OR THE FIRE STATION DONATION BASKET.
THE FOAMING MADNESS BEHIND THEM IS OVERSHADOWING
THE CAFFEINATED BANTER OF MEETING FOR THE FIRST TIME.

WHEN HE CAME IN THE BACK DOOR,
HE WAS WEARING A PIN STRIPE SUIT,
LEAVING HIS JACKET BY THE CHAIR,
BUT, NOW FROM THE LAST GLANCE, HE HAS CHANGED
INTO JEANS, STILL WEARING HIS STACEY ADAMS INTERVIEW SHOES
AND HIS SHIRT IS NOW LOOSELY UNBUTTONED, HAVING LOST
THE TIE IN THE MESSENGER BAG HE CARRIED WITH HIM;
SITTING COMFORTABLY, HE READS THE LOCAL NEWS.

AND THE HOMELESS MAN IS BACK, PICKING UP THE SCRAPS
OF SCONES AND FOLDING NEWSPAPER PAPER BOATS.
MAYBE IT WILL RAIN
AND HE CAN SAIL HIS SHIPS
DOWN THE 39TH STREET GUTTERS.

YOU, ME AND THE THIRD DEGREE BURNS

Speaking from the one who knows better
and for the one who never learns –

You
Me
And the third degree
Burns

If I tell you a secret,
Will you promise to keep it?

If I promise a dirty confession
Will you be smiling then?
Hoping you taught me a lesson
Taking me down from a high
That was not yours
Was not mine

Perversion's progression
Starts with the mind
Slithers in
Tickling and tantalizing
The skin

Ooh baby do and oh baby don'ts

Kissing, licking with closed eyes and doors
Will she or won't she
Keep asking
For more

COMPULSION IS HUNGER
AND YOU WERE STARVING
LONG BEFORE YOU EVER MET ME
THERE'S NOTHING ENTICING
ABOUT OBSESSION

YOU'RE STANDING NERVOUS, PERSPIRING
HOLDING ALL YOUR MONEY OUT
READY TO BET, WATCHING WORDS SPIN ROUND
THE ROULETTE WHEELS OF YOUR TURBULENT MIND
WHO'S LUCKY NUMBER IS IT?
YOURS, OR WAS IT MINE?

I THOUGHT I TOLD YOU
I DON'T PLAY THE FIELD
I LIKE TO BREAK (CRACKS DICE)
EVEN

I'M SURE THAT I'VE MENTIONED
AS QUEENS WERE CONCERNED -
IT WAS ONLY IN A DECK OF CARDS,
I DON'T NEED YOU TO CROWN ME

LUCK BE A LADY TONIGHT
(AND FRANKLY
WE'RE NOT SURE SHE WAS TO BEGIN WITH)
BUT AMONG THE BITCHES
I'M PRETTY SURE
YOU PREFER
MY PET
AGREE?

THE ACADEMY

My friends have all graduated head of their class
What was powder on a mirror or empty CD case
Turns into glass,
Burning sinuses or brimming over
In sweet smelling clouds

What was calming in capsule form is now distinguished
As China's only Caucasian
And if you're not fond of China,
You can call the Mexicans to cover up the potholes
On the streets of your arms

If you're scared of needles or can't tie a bow
You can smoke brown stripes off
Reynolds finest invention
RJ discloses it on his cigarettes
The common denominator isn't in their name
(it's the tar)

In our youth,
We were misplaced, misunderstood, and full of raw talent
Smoking cigarettes by the fences of our high schools,
Cutting classes, breaking all the rules
Thinking of time confined in hourglasses,
The grains of sands
Poured through like molasses
As young adults we sought our passions
In fruitless love affairs
Leaving us desperate
Often clinging to despair

WE FOUND COMFORT
IN SOCIAL SETTINGS THAT REQUIRED
SMALLER GATHERINGS WITHIN
A ROOM SECTIONED OFF FOR A FEW
TO COME IN AND OUT OF
A LITTLE LIGHTER THAN BEFORE

WE WERE KINGS AMONG PEASANTS
AND QUEENS AMONG A DECK OF CARDS
IN NIGHT CLUBS WE WERE GODS
OUR EGOS FILLED LIKE THE BALLOONS
THAT WE SUCKED DOWN WITH MIND-WARPING SPEED

WE NEVER STOOD IN LINE AT THE DOOR,
WE NEVER PAID FOR A DRINK

THE BARTENDERS KNEW US AND LOVED US
IF THE BOOKIES GOT PAID,
IT WAS BECAUSE WE MADE THE SCORE

WE RULED
WHEN DOWNTOWN WAS AN ESCAPE ROUTE
FOR UNDERAGE TEENAGERS TO DESTROY
STEM CELL OPPORTUNITIES
OFFERING RACE CARS IN THE FORM OF MITSUBISHI-E
AND TWO DOLLAR TRIPS FOR AN EIGHT HOUR TOUR

WE HOSTED THE AFTER PARTIES THAT RAGED INTO THE SUNLIGHT,
YELLING *TIMBER!* WHEN HE FELL
WE EGGED ON THE EGOS THAT LED TO THE FIGHTS

WE SHARED STORIES, INTERRUPTING ONE ANOTHER
TO GET THE LOUDEST LAUGH;

PASSING THE CONCH FOR ATTENTION...
THEY WERE MY SCOUTS,
AND I WAS THEIR DEN MOTHER
YOU COULDN'T HAVE ASKED FOR MORE
(BUT YOU ALWAYS DID)

OVER TIME, IT WAS AGE THAT SEPARATED US
DISTINGUISHING OUR DEGREES AMONGST EACH OTHER,
OUR EDUCATION WAS PAID ON A LOAN THAT WAS IN DEFAULT,
WE SUFFERED COLLECTORS AND HARASSING PHONE CALLS,
AND ALONG THE LINE,
WE'D FOUND ADDICTIONS THAT DESTROYED TRUST,
INFLICTIONS THAT WE'D YET TO DISCOVER
WOULD DESTROY THE COMMONALITY WE SHARED;
SUDDENLY, THERE WAS NO ROOM
WE'D ALL GONE INTO TOGETHER;
SOMEHOW, WE'D ALL COME OUT ALONE
AND PERHAPS THE TIME HAD COME
FOR US TO MOVE OUT OF THE DORM
FACE LIFE AND TO GET BACK INTO SOCIETY.

BUT WE STILL SHARED ONE THING IN COMMON,
NONE OF US,
NOT ONE OF US,
COULD FACE THE THOUGHT OF—
SOBRIETY

CRAMMED INN HEROIN TALES

HE GETS THE PORTLAND RAINS
STAYS IN FOR DAYS
GETTING THE HEROIN
DRIP
DRIP
DRIP
WELL, IF YOU HAVE TO COME DOWN
AT LEAST IT DRAINS

SMACK SMACK SMACK
HE FEELS THE PAIN
SHE SAYS,
IF YOU WANTED TO WEAR THE PANTS AROUND HERE,
YOU SHOULDA PUT YOUR BELT AROUND YOUR WAIST,
NOT YOUR ARM, DUMB BELL

HE SAYS,
YOU'RE GOING TO THE MOON! ALICE,
HIS FIST TIGHTENS UP
ARM VEERS UP SHE GETS SICK, RALPH!

IT'S PUNCTURED NOW
ZOOM ZOOM ZOOM
TWO ROCKET SCIENTISTS ON A BUS
TO AN OUTER GALAXY
MAKING CANDLES OUT OF THEMSELVES
DRIPPING AND MELTING ALL
WAXY WANE LIKE

RACES

I WAS LOVE SICK
SPOONING YOU
TYING MYSELF UP
LIVING OFF OF INJECTIONS TOO GOOD
TO BE TRUE
COWGIRL JUNKIE
SICK GIRL YOU'RE THE MONKEY
I WANT SO BAD ON MY BACK
TAKE IT
ANY WHICH WAY
YOU COULD PUSH IT
BUT YOU DIDN'T

REGRET, HOW COULD I?
YOU CALL
I FALL
DOWN THE STAIRS

NO ONE EVEN LOOKS

I WAIT
PREPARED
TO SAY SOMETHING
SO YOU'LL NOTICE
MAYBE EVEN
REMEMBER
MY SEASON

IT'S ALRIGHT

YOU'RE A RACE HORSE
KEN
TUCK
EEEEEEEEEEEEE
DERBY
AND I CAN'T CATCH UP
SMART IF IT WAS
WOULDN'T JONES
AND PATCH IT MAY BE
DON'T HAVE DAN

FUCK ME

UNLIKELY HEROS AMONG UNSUAL SUSPECTS

MILD MANNERED HUMORIST AND ARTIST DASHES
INTO THE BATHROOM, INJECTS HIS COSTUME
AND COMES OUT CAPTAIN HEROIN,
HEY MAN, LIFT YOUR HEAD,
WE GOTTA GO OUT AGAIN!

SARDONIC POET AND SECRETARY BY DAY,
SHE INHALES THE PERFUME OF IMMORTALITY
LEAVING THE MIRROR A GRAINY FORMER SELF
STRAW BATON IN HAND,
SHE IS NOW PART OF THE SUPER HERO ALLEGIANCE,
CONCHETTA CRYSTAL HERE TO RESCUE YOU
FROM THE NEVER ENDING CERTAINTY OF YOUR DEMISE,

COME ON GUYS!

TRAINED IN THE STREETS OF WEST LA AND VENICE,
TAKEN FOR GRANTED AS JUNKIES OR SPEED FREAKS,
THEY CONQUER THE NIGHT WITH THEIR INTREPID POWERS
THAT BE...

MORTICOM.

ONE OF US (SPEED FREAK AND JUNKIES)

SHH.
HOLD YOUR FIRE.
PUT THAT SEROTONIN BACK WHERE YOU FOUND IT!

WE WALK THE MEDICINE CABINET STUMBLE.
YOU ARE ALL GLASS SHELVES, SHATTERING IN THE SINK,
STABBING THE BOTTOMS OF MY FEET. DAMN IT MAN,
YOU'VE GOT A CLUMSY DISTRIBUTION SYSTEM!

HE SHAKES THE BOTTLE,
THE OLD VENICE MATING CALL
AND I AM OUT ON THE TILES, EMBEDDED BY SPLINTERED
SHARDS OF GLASS.

I'VE BEEN BEGGING SOMEONE
TO REMOVE THIS PAIN, PET ME AND MAKE ME HUMAN
AGAIN BUT EVERYONE'S AFRAID OF THE THORN
IN THE LIONS PAW.

DANIEL, WHERE DID YOU GO?

YOU COULD HAVE TAMED ME BUT YOU
LEFT ME FOR DEAD, AND, WELL,
THAT'S QUITE ALRIGHT, I SUPPOSE.

HOW 'BOUT IT
MOVE THAT ROCK JESUS,
WE GOT PLACES TO GO AND IT'S BEEN THREE DAYS,
TIME TO GET OUT OF THIS DARK CAVE,
IT'S LOOKIN' LIKE A CRACK HOUSE.

THEY TOLD ME YOU WERE A JUNKIE,
THAT YOU HAD NOTHING FOR ME.

I THOUGHT I WAS AT THE CIRCUS
WHEN I SAW THE MONKEYS
AND SHORT OF A MIRACLE,
NOTHING WAS GOING TO SAVE ME.

I WAS PART OF THE CARNIVAL,
THE ONE WISE TO THE GRIFT,
STARING OUT OF THE CORNER OF MY EYE,
MAKING THEM ALL NERVOUS, (AS *THEIR PEANUT SHELLS SHIFTED,*
WHILE THEY NICKLED AND DIMED THE GOLDFISH
TOSSING THE BALL INTO THE BASKET)
THEY WATCHED ME BACK,
WITH SNEERS,
BEADY EYES AS IF I WAS A NARC
OR SOMETHING.

I REMAINED STILL
ON THE WIRE, I CAUGHT THE TRAPEZE
GLIDING ELEGANTLY THROUGH THE AIR,
I YELLED *TRUST FALL!*
AND WHEN I LET GO AND YOU WERE NOWHERE TO BE FOUND.

IT WAS A LONG SEARCH TO SKY
BEFORE I HIT THE GROUND, VERTEBRAE, RIBS AND BONES CRACKED,
IT LEFT ME A BLOODY MESS.

I CRAWLED OUT FROM UNDER THE SPOTLIGHT,
ELBOWS THROUGH DIRT,
TRYING TO AVOID THE CLOWNS,
WITH THEIR FUCKING PISTOL FLOWERS,

AND THEIR ENORMOUS RED SHOES STEPPING ON MY FINGERS.
THOSE FUCKERS WERE POURING OUT BY THE DOZENS
AND THEY CAME OUT OF THE TINIEST CAR,
LIKE STEREO-TYPED BOLLYWOOD INDIANS,
OR MEXICANS FROM AN OLD DODGE CARAVAN
AT SANTA MONICA BEACH.

SAVAGES, I TELL YOU.
I WAS HUMAN CANOEING PAST
THE WHIPS, THE LOBSTER CLAWED POET,
THE BEARDED LADY WHO WAS SO CERTAIN OF HERSELF,
SHE BECAME A MUSICIAN,
THE STRONG MAN WAS DROPPING WEIGHTS
AND SENDING MERCURY UP THE NEEDLE
FOR A CUIPIE DOLL PRIZE,
THE SIAMESE TWINS HAD SPIT PERSONALITIES
THAT WERE DEFINITELY OUT TO GET ME, ALL THE WHILE THE
CROWD WAS LAUGHING IN THE BLEACHERS

I LEFT A MESSAGE AT YOUR TENT.

YOU WERE FAST
ASLEEP
WOKE UP AND TOLD ME NOT TO TRUST
THE WEATHER MAPS AND THAT WE WOULDN'T NEED
BRAKE LIGHTS IN THE DESERT. I NODDED, LIMPLY.
*NO ONE IS THERE TO SEE YOU, NO ONE SHOULD FOLLOW
THAT CLOSE ANYWAY...*
I COULDN'T HELP BUT AGREE.

PULLING BACK
ON THE CURTAIN,
THE ROUNDED LIGHTS SQUARED THE MIRROR,

FRAMING YOUR PROFILE
WHILE YOU NODDED, OUT.

I COULD SEE NOW,
FROM THE BOTTOM OF YOUR HEELS,
LOOKING HORIZONTALLY THE DIRT BENEATH YOUR FEET,
ON THE FRINGE OF A PERSIAN RUG
BY THE SWEEP OF MY DEBRIS,
PARADOXICAL AS IT WERE THAT
I WAS ACTUALLY LOWER THAN THE REST OF THE FREAKS.

WAS IT THE INABILITY TO BEND MY KNEES,
UNABLE TO STAND UP FACE TO FACE WITH YOU?
WAS IT THE BROKEN RIBS, MAKING MY ARMS
STIFF AND STUCK AT MY SIDE,
UNABLE TO BLOCK THE BRICKS,
OR THE WAY I TILTED,
LEANING TO THE FLOOR,
UNABLE TO KEEP A STRAIGHT LACE OR USE MY SPINE?

OR WAS IT YOU, THE HYPNOTIST, THE MIMIC ARTIST,
THE TATTOOED FREAK,
OR PERHAPS THE IDEA OF YOU
IN TUXEDO TAILS AND A TOP HAT?

OH MAN,
MY HEAD RINGS,
LEAPING AND TAKING IT TO THE HOOP,
I HAVE PERFORMED UNDER THREAT,
TO BE LEFT WAYSIDE AT THE TRACKS,
OR SHOWCASED IN THE BACK,
WHERE ONLY THE VENTRILOQUIST SPEAKS,
AND WHILE I CRACKED,

SEAMS WIDE OPEN,
I WAS LUCKY,
TO HAVE BEEN SEWN UP
AND STITCHED FOR THIS OCCASION
I'M READY TO BECOME ONE
OF YOU, DOUBLING BY THREES,
PART OF THE BROKEN DOWN SPEED FREAKS AND JUNKIES,
CHANTING,
ONE OF US,
ONE OF US

GLASS PIPES

AWKWARDNESS FILLED THE SPACE,
I SAT GAZING IN. (THE OUTSIDER.)

I FELL DISTANT IN VAGUE MEDITATION
LISTENING TO THEM TALK IN SPLINTERED OCTAVES
PLACING VALUE IN THEIR DISGUISED INTENTIONS,
SLYLY SEEKING RECOGNITION TO THE PLATED TRINKETS
TARNISHING BENEATH THE SHINE
THAT LAY BEFORE YOU AS OFFERING.

YOU SIT LIKE A QUIET BUDDHA,
INCENSE TRAILS ALL AROUND YOU,
AN ELECTRICAL HUM SOFTLY CHANTING
IN THE BACKGROUND.

THEY WAIT FOR ENLIGHTENMENT.
THEY STRETCH CASUALLY, YAWNING
IN EXHAUSTED WAVES OF FRUSTRATION.
THEY PULSE AT YOUR EVERY MOVEMENT,
DISORGANIZED, SELFISH AND INSECURE.

THEY SCULPT THE AWKWARD TENSION WITH BARE HANDS.
THEY DIVIDE THE ROOM,
FRAGMENTING SENSES BIT
BY BLOWN GLASS BLISTERED BIT
UNTIL THE CONVERSATION BECOMES MOSAIC.

I SENSE CONTENTMENT DERAILED,
A NEW DAY HAS APPROACHED,

LEAVING ME TO WALK BLINDLY
INTO THE SUN BLEACHED AFTERNOON
WHILE YOU REMAIN
INSIDE,
BEHIND SHADES OF PERCEPTION
EXISTING
AGAINST NATURE.

I WANT TO BE MORE CRYPTIC

I WANT TO BE
MORE
MYSTERY
LIKE A
SILENT MOVIE.
YOU KNOW, CONSIDERED UNPREDICTABLE,
FOREVER UNSOLVED,
POSSIBLY NOTED AS
A WONDER
OF THE WORLD.

I WANT TO BE
KNOWN
IN WORDS BUT
WITHOUT SOUND;
QUOTED ALONGSIDE
CONFUCIUS, CHURCHILL
OR, WELL, I'D HAPPILY SETTLE
JUST PLAIN MEMORABLE.

I WANT TO BE
SORTED IN ALPHABETICAL
ORDER.

I WANT TO BE
GREAT, MISUNDERSTOOD
LIKE TOP FORTY SONG LYRICS
OF ALL TIME, OR SCHIZOPHRENIC LOGIC,
GREEK LANGUAGE, SOMETHING

BEYOND THE AVERAGE
MEAN.

I WANT TO HEAR
BACK ECHOES OF THE TERMS
RIVETING, INTRIGUING, GRIPPING,
ARRESTING, ALLURING,
I WANT TO BE
REMEMBERED
AS FETCHING
WHILE MAINTAINING DEADPAN WIT,
CHARM, SENSITIVITY
THOUGHTFULNESS
AND BEING INFECTIOUS.

I WANT TO SAY LESS.

WHEN

I miss the feeling—
being held close to chest,
thumb over lashes and pushing back
the excess of curls that hide my face.
Oh to become part of the far off stare
that eventually blurs
in your arms,
after my eyes stop
climbing the walls,
where the window
offers peace and the trees with long branches weep
against the ground like rain.
I want to feel that, maybe
just once more again.

BEATBACK COVER

CAN'T PICK UP THE PHONE TODAY
I SEE, CLEARLY
THE UNGRATEFUL DISPLAY,
LIKE CHEAP ARTWORK
AT A CHURCH BIZARRE...

LAST WEEK-
YOU WERE HAPPY TO HAVE
YOUR FINGERS KNUCKLE DEEP
DRAGGING IN MY HONEY

I GET YOU
YOU'RE JUST A CREEP
BACK INTO MY LIFE,
SIDESWIPE,
LEAVE ME
BE
TYPE.

IF WE ONLY HAD GROUPIES WE'D BE SET

HE'S AT THE WILSHIRE ROYALE,
NO HEAT, NO AIR CONDITIONING
BUT THEY GOT LOW RENT
TWO TWIN BEDS AND A POOL.

YOU CAN WATCH THE TOURISTS ROLLERBLADE
DOWN THE SUNLIT STREET,
THE WOULD BE MODELS,
ALMOST ACTRESSES IN ALL THEIR
PRETTY GIRL SUN GLASSED PHASES.

HE'S TAKING A LONG SHOWER,
SHOOTIN' DOPE WHILE THE WATER RUNS—

HE'S WEARING A SHIRT WITH DEVIL EMBLEMS
ON THE BUTTONS,
JUST OPEN ENOUGH TO TAN HIS CHEST,
HE SITS IN THE LOUNGE CHAIR,
FALLING ASLEEP UNDER PALM TREES AND
HE'S CALIFORNIA DREAMING,
WHILE ALL HIS LEAVES ARE TURNING
BROWN.

HE'S SMOKING THE GLASS PIPE
TO THAT PERFECT
MILKY WHITE INFERNO
WHILE HE GIVES HIS BEST DENIRO FACE, TELLING JOKES,
AND THERE'S PROBABLY A HER I'D HATE TO MEET
DRIPPING AROUND HIM,

STRETCHING HER THIN ARMS
EXTENDING EVERY INCH OF SELF HATE SHE HAS
ON THE BED WITH JUNKIE PATIENCE
WAITING FOR HER TURN.

I OFFERED HIM A GREYHOUND TICKET

BUT HE ASKED ME TO WIRE THE MONEY

I KNEW THEN,
SAME AS BEFORE,
I'D LOST AGAIN,

THERE WAS NO FIX
I COULD OFFER HIM.

DIRECTIONS TO REVOLUTION BOULEVARD

HE CALLS ME LATE AT NIGHT,
HE'S DRUNK AND I BET HE'LL STAY UP
'TIL THAT DIRTY SUN MAKES ITS DEBUT OVER TIJUANA,
PUNCTURING THE COMFORT IN HIS LINE OF SIGHT.

HE TELLS ME THERE'S SOMETHING ABOUT ME HAUNTING HIM.

HE SLOPPILY SPILLS HIS REMORSE ONTO THE TABLE
SLURRING PROMISES, DRIFTING AWAY –
COMING BACK AGAIN, TO SAY
THERE'S JUST SOMETHING ABOUT YOU

HE SAYS I KNOW IT'S TRUE,
HE'S NOT THE ONLY ONE,
TO HAVE CONFESSED THIS —
HE SAYS HE DOESN'T KNOW WHAT IT IS
THEN, HE CONTRADICTS HIMSELF,
TELLING ME I DESERVE TO KNOW
WHAT IT IS THAT MAKES THEM ALL LOVE ME SO —
HE SAYS IT WAS MY EYES,
CAPTIVATING, FELINE
BRIMMING IN THE COLOR OF ENVY.

HE OVER SATURATES THE COMPLIMENT
BY SAYING HE WANTS TO BE IN ME
MY SILENCE FOLDS HIM AGAIN WITH REGRET,

IF I WOULD JUST GO TO MEXICO,
HE PROMISES,
HE'LL REPAY THE DEBT.

TIJUANA TAXI

WHEN I SUGGESTED THAT THEY
MIGHT WANT HIM DEAD, HE SAID
PEOPLE CAN WANT A LOT OF THINGS.

HE'S BREATHLESS WALKING
THROUGH ALLEY DARKNESS DRESSED IN POTHOLES
LITTERED WITH TIN CANS,
FENCES, I CAN HEAR
SOUNDS OF BARKING GREYHOUNDS,

HE'S ONLY GOT TWENTY MINUTES
TO SPILL IT ALL TO ME, PROMISING
I WAS BETTER OFF NOT KNOWING.

ONE DAY ONE DAY
THE LIGHTHOUSE BLINKS
UNTIL THE TURNSTILE FADES ROUND AWAY,
COMING BACK TO SAY,
SHINING WORDS IN HOPELESS SKIES
THAT FOGGILY FOLLOW ME OVER
THE BAJA SAND FLEA SHORES,
PAST THE CORNCOB WEBS OF CARELESS PICNICS,
OR ROWS MULTI PASTEL FLAVORS OF CHICLETS,

COME AND VISIT, IT'LL BE THE LAST TIME,
YOU KNOW, BEFORE I'M DEAD.

TIJUANA HAS CHANGED
IMAGINE, CHICAGO

BOOTLEGGING 1930S,
MUSCLING, GOING FOR RANK

EIGHT FOOLS OUT LAST WEEK

THEY WERE GONNA TAKE OUT THIS GUY
LIVING AT MY PAD, A HEAVY HITTER

TALKED THE MINUTE MADE MAN
OUT OF IT, DONATED CASH
DONE, DEAD LOLA DEAD

    LEAVE HIM BEHIND, SIRENS SAID.

HE'S GETTING PICKED UP
IN A SUIT,
RANTING ABOUT THE MOONSHINE
IN THE BATHTUBS, BEGGING ME
TO BRING JACK DANIELS,
PLAY SWITCHBOARD TO HIS SCOREBOARD
AND PASS THE WORD,
HE'S IN

TAR FILLED WASTELAND,
FECES IN THE BREEZE,
IT'S EASY HE TELLS ME,
I JUST TOOK OUT THE COMPETITION

I REMIND HIM, IT ALWAYS COMES BACK,
BIGGER AND BETTER AND PREPARED.

HIS RICHES INCLUDE AN AK 47,
HIS OWN APARTMENT,

NOE'S UNCLE WAS THE EPICENTER,
IT TURNED OUT
AND THEY DIDN'T EVEN KNOW IT.
I CAN PICTURE THE WHITE SPIT GATHERING
IN THE CORNERS OF HIS MOUTH,
HE IS SHUDDERING IN TWITCHING CONVERSATION
AND THE RECEPTION IS STARTING TO GET LOST
THROUGH THE TURNS OF HIS RAPID CONFESSION.

HE SAYS IOWA?
    NO, FOOL, KANSAS CITY
HE SAYS, YOU FELL IN LOVE WITH SOMEONE?
INTERUPTS WITH DID HE GET YOU. ...
    NO, NOT YET.
THEN HE STIFLES ME,
HE'S ONLY GOT TWENTY MINUTES,
HE'S NOT INTERESTED IN MY BEGINNINGS.
HE'S TOO NEAR THE EDGE, THE CLIMATIC END
READY FOR THE SWAN DIVE FALL,

I'LL BE ON THE INTERNATIONAL LINE
WAITING FOR THE RINGING OF THE LONG DISTANCE
CALL FROM HIS MOTHER THROUGH THE OPERATOR
CURSING AT THE CHARGES,
ASKING HOW MUCH FOR BAIL, SHE'LL CRY
AND WHEN SHE TELLS ME NO, NOT THE JAIL, BUT THE MORGUE,
SHE'LL SAY THEY PICKED HIM UP IN A TJ TAXI,
DROPPED HIM OFF SOMEWHERE,
AND HE NEVER CAME
HOME.

LIVING AFTER WE DIE

ALMOST ONLY COUNTS
IN HORSESHOES AND MAYBE POOL SHOTS
AIN'T NO WINNING FOR LOSING

SO, HERE WE ARE

MY BEST FRIEND AND ME, STANDING
TIJUANA DOORWAYS,
SMOKING CIGARETTES
STARING INTO EACH OTHERS EYES THROUGH
A DRUG-ALCOHOL INDUCED HAZE,
THAT KEPT US UP ALL NIGHT TALKING,
I THOUGHT I'D NEVER SEE YOU AGAIN

I'M AFRAID IF I LEAVE NOW,
I MIGHT NOT EVER COME BACK,
BUT I LIE AND SING ALONG
NO, WILD HORSES COULDN'T DRAG ME AWAY
WHILE YOU PUT YOUR ARM
AROUND MY SHOULDERS,
WE SWAY SAD IN OUR SONG
WE COULD TRAVEL TO TECATE
BUT IT CAN'T CHANGE THE CHOICES WE'VE MADE

I SAY I'M TIRED,
I SEE YOU NODDING
IN AGREEMENT,
AND WAIT TILL YOU SLEEP
ONE MORE PROMISE
I COULDN'T KEEP

TIJUANA GENERAL (A CASE OF STAPH, MRSA, A STROKE AND A COMA, *PLACE YOUR BETS*)

IT ISN'T SIMPLE ANYMORE, YOU KNOW,
CROSSING BORDERS TO VISIT YOU,
THE STREETS THAT WERE ONCE CARNIVAL COLORS,
WHERE WE PAINTED THE TOWN RED,
ARE ALL DARK, THEY LOOK DIFFERENT,
EVERYTHING FAMILIAR IS FOREIGN AND UNSAFE.

YOU'RE LAYING ON A COT IN THE HALL
OF TIJUANA GENERAL HOSPITAL, COMATOSE,
LISTENING TO THE DOCTORS BETTING ON YOUR
LIFE EXPECTANCY AND FROM WHAT YOU HEAR,
IT ISN'T LOOKING GOOD.

I HAVE BEEN HANGING ON THE LINE,
THE ONLY FRIEND YOU HAVE
WITH A PASSPORT OR IS LEGALLY ALLOWED
TO TRAVEL OUT OF STATE
THEY TOLD ME YOU HAD HOURS TO LIVE
AND IT'S GOING ON THE THIRD DAY.
DON'T WORRY, I CALLED YOUR MOM,
I'M ON MY WAY TO SAY GOODBYE.

I MEET HER AT THE *7-11* ON SEPULVEDA,
IN THE PARKING LOT WHERE THE FLUORESCENT BULBS
MAKE EVEN SOBER PEOPLE FEEL CRACKED OUT,
SHE PULLS UP IN A TOYOTA TERCEL CIRCA *1987*
STUFFED TO THE GILLS WITH EVERYTHING

YOU MIGHT NEED, SHE'S BEEN ALL OVER WEST LA
TAKING DONATIONS OF CLOTHING, FOOD, MEDICATIONS,
WHATEVER BOUNTY SHE COULD FIND
TO DROP LIKE THE RED CROSS AT YOUR HOUSE.

I SEE THE GHOST OF YOUR FATHER,
HE LOOKS DEEPLY INTO WHO I AM, TO THE CORE OF ME,
AND WITH HIS REGAL ACCENT HE SAYS, MY WIFE,
SHE SAYS I MUST MEET YOU, I DON'T KNOW WHY.
I UNDERSTAND YOU SAVED MY SON
AND HE LOVES YOU VERY MUCH,
BUT YOU ARE NOT WITH HIM.
AND GERARDO LEFT IT AT THAT FOR YEARS,
BURNING QUESTIONS DEGREES UNTIL IT SET FIRE
AND HE WOULD BURN ALIVE
BLOCKS FROM YOU.

I AM WITH YOUR MOTHER, SHE'S YELLOW,
HER LIVER IS FAILING, AND WOULDN'T YOU KNOW
ONE PILL CURES THE WORLD NOW —
AND SHE'S TOO LATE, BECAUSE OF THE NEEDLE
AND THE DAMAGE DONE,
SHE'S SUFFERING BECAUSE OF YOU AND YOUR OLD MAN,
I REMEMBER HOW HE LOVED NEIL YOUNG,
THE RADIO QUIETLY PLAYING YOUR FUNERAL PRELUDE,
I SHAKE OFF THE IMPENDING DOOM I FEEL
YOUR MOTHER TELLS ME THEY SAID
YOU ONLY HAD HOURS LEFT,
COMPLICATIONS FROM TAKING IT IN THE NECK
ONE TOO MANY TIMES,
YOU WERE IN A COMA, YOU HAD A STROKE AS A RESULT
SHE LOOKS AT ME WITH HER BEAUTIFUL
WATERING BLUE EYES AND BEGS ME

Tell me it's not true, that my son is not a thief.
And I said, you never took nothing from anyone
that didn't have it coming.

She says you are her miracle, she prayed all night,
and she knew when you awoke,
she didn't tell you I was coming,
she promised too many times
and you wouldn't believe her anyway.

I want to find the jukebox
that took our spare dollar bills,
unrolled, three songs always starting with *Bad Fish*,
Creep and depending on who was nearby
maybe *Maggie* or *Dean Martin*
and we would take the eightball to the corner
and sink it,
we would fall asleep midconversation,
we were ever-so-cool
down Venice Boulevard,
up to the Malibu Shore, Hollywood Hills —
our reputations superseded our decay.

I want to go back to our apartment in Venice,
where we would get up for work
by throwing the alarm clock at each other
instead of pressing snooze,
mad dashing for the shower.
I remember the episodes of M.A.S,H.
droning on the tiny TV while you snored
so loudly I thought I would die —
and I forced myself to hear the ocean
or the rain on the sand.

I WANT TO SHARE A COKE WITH YOU,
THE ONLY WAY WE CAN,
WITH A SMILE.

THEY SAID I SAVED YOU THREE OR FOUR TIMES,
THEY SAID YOU LOVED ME
BUT I KNOW THEY BLAME ME FOR YOUR DEBT.

IT WAS NEVER ENOUGH MY FRIEND.
ALL THOSE WILD HORSES,
ALL THOSE WILD HORSES
TIJUANA HAS CHANGED SINCE THE LAST TIME
WE WERE DRUNK AND SWAYING IN DOORWAYS
I DON'T UNDERSTAND ANYMORE WHY YOU CAN'T COME BACK.

WHY WE DIDN'T SOBER UP,
WHY THERE ARE NO BABIES AND IT FEELS LIKE GRAVES
EVERYWHERE I WALK AND TIP-TOE PAST,
WHERE ARE YOU? BEFORE THE BORDER, FLOOD LIGHTS
GATE THE ENTRY, CAMERAS MECHANICALLY FOLLOW
PLATES ENTRANCE TO EXIT PASSPORTS TO LINES,
WALKING HOURS ON PAVEMENT COVERED IN DRY DIRT
YOUR MOTHER TAKES THE WHEEL AT THE ENTRY,
SHE SHOWS ME WHERE YOUR FATHER DIED, MYSTERIOUSLY,
SHE TELLS ME OF THE DOGS BEING POISONED, YOUR BLACKIE,
WAS FOUND UNDERNEATH THE HOUSE, PINNED IN FEAR
BY THE FIRE. WE TURN INTO YOUR CASA
AND I AM TERRIFIED TO SEE YOU.

SHE SAYS, *ERIK, I BROUGHT YOU A SURPRISE.*
YOU ARE IN A HOSPITAL BED, FACING THE WALL,
TEMPER-PEDIC BACK TO ME, AND WITHOUT MISSING A BEAT
YOU SAY *JENKINS?*

I RUN UP TO YOUR BEDSIDE AND WEEP,
YOU PUT YOUR FRAIL ARM AROUND ME AND SAY
WHAT UP CREEPY?
I LAUGH AND REPLY,
NOTHING CRAWLY.

WE TALK ALL NIGHT.
YOU COUGH CONSTANTLY, LUNG CAPACITY IS SHOT,
BUT IT DOESN'T MATTER, I WILL SIT THROUGH
THE SKIN CRAWLING FEAR OF CATCHING
WHATEVER IT IS YOU DRAGGED OUT OF THE DEAD WITH YOU,
TO SAVE THIS.

I GET TO THE BORDER, ESCORTED BY YOUR COUSIN
WHO ADMITS, *I THINK I DRANK TOO MUCH,
CAN YOU WALK IT FROM HERE?*

I CATCH A GREYHOUND BACK TO LOS ANGELES WITH MY LAST $25,
I DON'T EVEN HAVE BUS FARE
FROM DOWNTOWN TO HOME AND I BEG THE RTD DRIVER
TO LET ME ON THE BUS BY SKID ROW
WHEN I ARRIVE SHORTLY AFTER AT 12AM,
SURROUNDED BY PIMPS
AND ANGRY ADDICTS LIKE VULTURES.

I GET HOME AND THINK ABOUT YOU.

I WILL TELL EVERY LIE YOU NEED TO HEAR
TO MAKE YOU CROSS OVER AGAIN.

STRIDULATION

December in Los Angeles,
The crickets are stroking their legs,
The prime time repeats are glowing from the windows
Of the lonely bedrooms lined along the side streets
Off Venice or Sepulveda Boulevards.
The sky is scraped by the planes coming into LAX,
Business men, exiting briskly to the street,
Black cars to four star hotels,
While broken hearted women dragging children home,
After moving again, cry on their uncle's shoulder,
The cars are all parked, right up to the red,
The alarms are all set to get up before
The street cleaning between 8 and 10 am,
The gardners are all tucked in,
Before the gas-blowing disruption, moves the leaves
From one drive way to the other again
And the daycares are all closed,
The shrieks and wheels on gravel sounds are silent,
But the cricket can't sleep?
It's chirping, nocturnal creatures that they are,
Rubs its legs together
Hoping to tether another,
While I stroke
The keys.

OMERTA

I COULD HEAR THE MUSIC,
STATIONS OVERLAYING ONE ANOTHER.
A RUGGED DRUM BEAT,
A CAROUSEL OF SOUNDS,
THEN A SIREN SINGING AND SWISH,
IT WOULD CHANGE AGAIN
BUT THIS TIME IT WASN'T MUSIC,
ONLY FORMS OF MY LIFE.

AS IF A DJ WAS SELECTING THE RECORDS
AND THE SONGS WERE THE BEATS AND SWISH,
THE BEAT WAS STILL, THEN IT STARTED AGAIN
AND I COULDN'T HOLD MY THOUGHTS TOGETHER.

I WAS THINKING THOUGHTS
AND THESE MINISCULE THOUGHTS HAD NO IDEA,
THEY HAD NO WORDS WITH DEFINITIONS
LIKE HOLLOW MEMORY ON A SCALE,
I COULD SEE INSIDE THE POSTCARD OR DOWN THE SIDEWALK
BUT COULD NOT FILL THE ROOM WITH FURNITURE,
THE LETTERS HAD NO SIGNATURE,
THE PERSON IN THE DREAM
WAS NOT THE PERSON
PHYSICALLY SPEAKING
BUT THEIR FACE REPRESENTED SOMEONE
I COULD NOT SEE OR DID NOT KNOW
AND YET WAS ALL TOO FAMILIAR WITH
IN THE PAST OR REMINISCENT FUTURE.

THE SADNESS IN THE ROOM REACHED THE CEILING
AND WEPT FROM THE CORNERS
IN TONES OF MARMALADE LIGHT,
STICKYING AND STAINING THE ROOM,
MAKING IT IMPOSSIBLE TO LEAVE.

TWO SONGS UNDONE AT THE SAME TIME.
TWO WORDS THAT DID NOT INTERSECT
AT ALL BUT SUDDENLY TWISTED INTO CANE.
TWO MANY TIMES, TOO MUCH LIKE BEFORE,
AND NOW THE STATIC WAS ELECTRIC,
PULLING SINGLE STRANDS OF MY HAIR INTO THE AIR,
LEAVING ME MAGNETICALLY ATTRACTED TO THE FLOOR
AND MY EYES CLOSED,
I COULD SEE THE SCOPES RANGING
IN THE DISTANCE AND CLOSING IN ON NOTHING
WHILE MAKING PERFECT PICTURE FRAMES
FOR DESTRUCTION.

PART TWENTY-TWO:
A LA RECHERCHE DU TEMPS PERDU

I HAVE WORN YOU LIKE OUTDATED PEARLS.
WAITING FOR A BYGONE ERA SOMEWHERE IN BETWEEN
A RAINY-DAY CAB RIDE IN NEW YORK CITY
AND THE BOGART GOOD-BYE
WHERE WE'LL ALWAYS HAVE PARIS.

I HAVE DRESSED IN SEQUINED GOWNS,
GLOVED HANDS TO ELBOWS, WAITING FOR YOUR INVITATION.
I HAVE WALKED MILES DRUNK IN HIGH HEELS
THROUGH CRACKED CREVICES OF SIDEWALKS
WE ONCE SWEET-HEARTED, HOLDING HANDS
AND PASSED IN DARK HOURS THROUGH THE PARKS
NOW, ALONE UNTIL I GOT HOME.

NO BEACON LIGHT,
NO NEW MESSAGES.

I HAVE PACKED YOU IN BOXES WITH OLD TROPHIES,
YEARBOOKS, BAD POETRY AND VARIOUS VERSIONS
OF MY NAME IN GRAFFITI ART.
I STILL OWN THE LED ZEPPELIN CASSETTES
YOU MADE ME WHEN THE BOX SET CAME OUT.
I STILL REMEMBER HOW YOU REWOUND
II BY HAND WITH A PENCIL SO I COULD HEAR
THANK YOU IN MUSIC CLASS IN 9TH GRADE.

I HAVE WORN YOU AROUND MY WRIST LIKE A WATCH
THAT IN NITELY LOSES TIME

AND BECAUSE I CANNOT AFFORD TO HAVE IT FIXED,
I AM FORCED TO ADJUST TO LATENESS OR STILL HOURS
IN WHICH TIME CONTINUES FORWARD

SOMEWHERE YOU ARE
AFFORDED CONTINUOUS MOTION;

WHILE I LIE STILL
FOREVER LAMENTING
ALL THE MEASUREMENTS LOST.

BABY-DADDY COMES TO MISSOURI

He arrived after midnight on a Greyhound bus;
There we were, Slyvie and me, waiting off Troost,
among doo-rags, socks in sandals, sweat pants,
junkie saliva, and a random guitarist,
hoping for a nickel.

When he got in my car,
she asked him if he had anything.

He said he'd gone sober, except for the weed
he pulled out of his pocket, smiling
without front teeth.

All he wanted was to see his baby in a plastic pool
she told me.

They made phone calls begging for money
to be wired to the nearest Walmart
with elaborate stories of starvation,
child related emergencies and promises that
of course, they would never pull such a scam on me.

He drank beers mid-morning, leaving cans
on the coffee table and would leave with Sylvie,
returning from garage sales
with tennis rackets, potpourri, jewelry
and bags of clothing, filling my house,
where neither of them had right to own much of anything,
throwing them into my foyer closet.

WHEN ALL THE WIRES ARRIVED
THEY TOOK A BUS AND CASHED IN.
INSTEAD OF BUYING MILK, DIAPERS, OR NECESSITIES
THEY WENT TO THE CASINO,
AS IF ON SOME MAGICAL VACATION
WHILE I WATCHED THE FOUR-MONTH-OLD CHILD
HE'D COME TO MEET

THEY LOST ALL BUT TWENTY DOLLARS.

SO, WITH NOTHING TO FEED THE BABY
AND NO CIGARETTES IN SIGHT,
THEY TROTTED DOWN TO THE LIQUOR STORE ON 39TH
AND BOUGHT $20 WORTH OF LOTTERY TICKETS,
AND WOULDN'T YOU KNOW IT,
THERE WASN'T A SCRATCHER AMONG THEM?

BABY-DADDY SHOWED NO SIGNS OF LEAVING,
THE TWO PLAYING HOUSE,
OFFERING THE BABY ICE CREAM AND SODA
BECAUSE DADDY WANTED HER TO TRY IT WITH HIM FIRST.

WASN'T IT DARLING?

SYLVIE, THAT EMPTY LITTLE GIRL THOUGHT SHE HAD
A FAMILY WITH HIM, A CONNECTION,
SOMEONE TO FILL A GAP FOR HER
FOREVER SEEKING A DADDY ROLE
SHE THOUGHT THIS PATHETIC TRAILER PARK SITUATION
WAS WHOLE.

AND IT WOULD OF COURSE BE ME
WHO DESTROYED IT FOR HER.

I HAD DECIDED THAT THE TIME HAD COME,
AND SO, WHEN THEY TOLD ME HE COULDN'T FLY BACK
TO THE GODFORSAKEN PLACE HE'D COME FROM
AND HIS FRIEND IN SOME DAKOTA
WAS NOWHERE NEAR NOR WOULD BE
TO COME GET HIM AS ONCE PLANNED,
WE ARRANGED FOR A BUS TICKET
WHICH SOMEHOW WASN'T AVAILABLE
FOR TWO DAYS IN A ROW
WHEN THEY TRIED TO PURCHASE IT.

I ARRANGED THE TICKET,
I DROVE HIM TO THE BUS STOP AGAIN,
WHILE LITTLE MISS CRIED HYSTERICALLY
AS IF PAID AT A FUNERAL TO WAIL
FOR THE LOSS OF A LOVED ONE.

ON THE WAY IN THE HOUSE, CROSSING THE FOYER
THAT SHE HAD CRAMMED FULL OF YARD SALE SHIT,
SHE TOSSED THE CARSEAT
(BABY IN TOW) ON THE FLOOR,
AND SCREAMED
ALL HE WANTED
WAS TO SEE HIS BABY IN A PLASTIC POOL!

I THINK IT'S A DAMN GOOD THING
THE BABY COULDN'T HOLD HER HEAD UP YET,
NOT TO SEE WHAT ALL I HAD WITNESSED.

THAT'S ALL I CAN SAY.

CHILDREN'S COURT: (MONTERREY PARK, CALIFORNIA)

EVERY WOMAN HERE HAS FLAWLESS
MANICURED OR TATTOOED EYEBROWS
RAISED SHARPLY ABOVE EYES GLARING
AT A ROOM FULL OF PEOPLE WHO CLEARLY OWE THEM.

THEY ALL HAVE MOTHER TEARS,
AND *I SWEAR I HAVEN'T* STATEMENTS IN COMPLETE DENIAL.

ARTS AND CRAFTS CHILDREN,
POOR WITH THEIR WORN OUT,
MOST PRIZED SHOES AND PRETTIEST BOWS
IN THEIR NEATLY COMBED HAIR.

SULLEN FACES WEARING
IT HAD TO COME TO THIS,
CAFETERIA LINE, CASH ONLY.

REBELLIOUS PROMISES COMPLIANCE
AN AFFIDAVIT OF LIES

SOME ARE EVEN HERE
WITH THE VERY MOTHERS WHO RAISED THEM.

ARMS CROSSED WITH I TOLD YOU SO LIPS PURSED,
COLD SHOULDERING THE PLEAS
OR RUBBING THE BACKS OF THEIR MIRROR IMAGES.
SOMEWHERE, NOT WITH THEM,
ARE THE CHILDREN WHO ARE WAITING
TO COME HOME.

(THE FOSTER) DAUGHTER

Her smile is filament to incandescence
Her laughter is carbonated in pastel,
painting the walls and tickling my ears.

Her words crinkle like tissue paper,
forming lacy sentences,
sometimes caught in a groove of parrot repetition,
she sounds
it
out.

Her eyes are cognoscente and wide,
spritely
in elevated moods
but when dark, those eyes stare through me,
past my soul,
where I can make no apology
for why she is here,
with me.

When she goes to sleep
I kiss her tender cheek, profess my love,
wishing her goodnight anxiously
waiting for tomorrow, just to be
with her again.

I cannot think,
I cannot stop
to think, this will someday end.

SAMANTHA MARIE

SHE HAS THE MOST BEAUTIFUL EYES,
OPEN WIDE,
WISE BEFORE HER TIME AND YOU CAN
SEE HER SOAK IN THE DEPTH
OF THE ROOM, SHE STARTLES ME BY ASKING
WHY ARE YOU CRYING?
I TELL HER I'M NOT AND CONTINUE
TO FOLD THE LAUNDRY, MATCH THE PATTERNS
TO HER PASTEL WARDROBE AND MAKE NEAT LITTLE PILES
ON THE BED, THEN SHE SAYS,
I SEE IT IN YOUR EYES.

SHE DOES NOT BELONG TO ME,
BUT SHE OWNS EVERY BIT
OF WHAT SOMETIMES FEELS LIKE MY WILL TO LIVE
IN THOSE TINY, CLUMSY, AND STICKY HANDS
THAT ARE ALWAYS REACHING OR GRABBING FOR SOME
ATTENTION;
OFTEN TIMES JUST SIMPLY TO HOLD MY HAND
WHILE CROSSING THE BUSY STREETS,
DANGEROUS PARKING LOTS, AND UNFAMILIAR PUBLIC
SPACES WHERE EVERYTHING IS TALL, WIDE, LONG
DISTANCES
AND REQUIRES ME TO CHAPERONE
SHE NEVER TRIES TO BREAK FREE
TO BE INDEPENDENT OF ME, EXPLORE THE WORLD BEYOND
OR VANISH BEHIND THE PILLARS, CLOTHING RACKS,
OR CAUGHT IN A REFLECTION IN THE MIRROR IN PASSING,
TRAPPED

By the person she identifies as herself.

I call her my love, my angel, my Kansas City Star,
She tells me she can't get dressed today,
Her crown broke then she changes her dress twice
To get that perfect twirl when spinning around
Hair in wispy pig tails,
Insisting on my violet perfume
To make her just perfectly ready.
She sits on my lap and she knows,
Today she goes back home,
She holds her locket with my picture
In the silver hollow hue,
And says whenever I open this
You are telling me that you love me,
And then she cries when I suggest clasping the heart,
 I don't want you to stop loving me.

She sings come rain or come shine
With me a cappella
Hands up high as a mountain,
And low deep as a river
As though she was behind a microphone.

SAMMIE, THE FIRST ONSET OF A MEMORY

THE NIGHT BEFORE SHE LEFT, I COULDN'T SLEEP.
I DIDN'T WANT IT TO END.

I WAS CONVINCED ONCE SHE WAS GONE
THAT HER TINY VOICE WOULD ECHO THROUGH THE HALLWAYS.

I REMOVED EVERY BIT OF HER PRESENCE
IN FUTILE EFFORT TO HIDE MY GRIEF.
I PAINTED THE WALLS RED AND PURPLE.

WHERE WE'D ONCE PANTONED OUR HOME TOGETHER,
I REPLACED HER PICTURES WITH ARTWORK
OR LEFT NAILS SPARSE AND BARREN IN HER ABSENCE

I WAS ENTIRELY WRONG ABOUT HER VOICE.

IT WAS THE SILENCE THAT FILLED THE HALLWAYS,
SUFFOCATING THE ROOMS WITHOUT HER
TO LET THE LIGHT, THE FRESH AIR
IT WAS UNBEARABLE.

I REALIZED A YEAR HAD PASSED AND SOON
THE MONTHS WOULD DISPLACE US UNTIL MORE TIME, SILENCE
AND DISTANCE WAS ALL THAT REMAINED IN THE CREVICES
AND WIDE SPACES SHE'D LEFT BEHIND.

IN THIS SILENT MOVIE, I REPLAY MY FATHER FIXING THE
ZIPPER TO HER HALLOWEEN COSTUME,
SAVING THE DAY AS ALWAYS
SO THAT SHE COULD DRESS UP AS A VELOUR MONSTER SHARK.

In this vision, she is walking with us
up and down Cheviot hills in wonderment
of the macabre displays, costumes
and can't wait to knock on another door.
She doesn't comprehend
the trick or treat rhythm at each destination,
doesn't understand why no one has invited her in
but the other children gather around her, follow her
and we watch her tire as the evening continues.
She is curled up in my fathers arms
walking with us back to the car
and then we are home.

I don't remember putting her to bed that night.

It's like the silence filling the room
that is eating away
at the shell of me.
A year ago, today

MR. DUMPTY'S APOLOGY IS REFUSED

THEY SAID THEY WEREN'T ACCEPTING MY APOLOGIES
BECAUSE I WAS TOO BROKEN ANYMORE,
I THOUGHT FRIENDS FORGAVE
THAT THEY ACCEPTED THE WHOLE ME,
EVEN IF I'M STITCHED UP LIKE A TIM BURTON DOLL
FULL OF PIECES OF STATIONARY WITH STAINED INK,
SHATTERED BUTTONS, SHAFTED ZIPPERS, PENCIL TIPS
AND PARTICLES OF WORDS I MEANT TO SAY,
PROMISES I MEANT TO KEEP,
INVITATIONS I MEANT TO RESPOND TO
AND GIFTS I NEVER OFFERED
THEY STILL RESIDE WHERE YOU NO LONGER
ACCEPT APOLOGIES,
ALL THE BROKEN PIECES OF ME.

WHEN *TAXI DRIVER* MEETS *FALLING DOWN*

EVENTUALLY, AFTER REALIZING NO ONE WAS LISTENING TO ME;
MENTALLY, WHILE THEY SPOKE
I STRUCK MATCHES,
TOSSING THE FLAMES EFFORTLESSLY
TOWARD THEM.

I STOOD AT THE END OF PIERS, THINKING
I DID EVERYTHING THEY TOLD ME TO DO.
I STARED DOWN STORIES AT INNOCENT BYSTANDERS
LIKE ANTS CROSSING STREETS
AND PUSHING ALONG PAVEMENT
CONTEMPLATING MY IMPACT.

I CROSSED BRIDGES ABOVE WATER,
LOOKING AT THE VACANT SIDE VIEWS
AND DARK UNDERBELLY OF THE BLACK SEA.

I STOPPED SHOWING UP TO WORK ON TIME,
I STOPPED CLEANING THE THOSE EVER-SO-DUSTY CORNERS
THAT DROVE ME MAD.
EATING WAS A CHORE,
DRINKING WAS A BLOATED EFFORT.

I WAS GREY ON GREY, MERGING LANES
ON A TRAFFIC INFESTED FREEWAY,
EXITING TO NOWHERE IN PARTICULAR,
LIVING A LIFE WITHOUT MEANING.

FUCKING, EATING, SLEEPING, STARING

At the 3am ceiling or crack of august
dawn window without feeling.

You did good they said

You tried your hardest

It's a broken system

And their words felt like insults
from a stranger, in a foreign tongue,
who accidentally spits on my lip during their
speech while my absent minded finger is
brushing off the rest of their uncontrollable saliva
gracefully using my sleeves for a handkerchief;
as they appear to question my subtle movements—
to indicate composure again,
or ruffled fighting feathers,
as I exited each experience blankly.

They compared their emotions
situations, solutions, therapy
and gave advice as prescribed pill bottles
of aspirin for me to swallow down
in handfuls, with luke-warm water,
cuing the headache and I doubted it
would ever end.

The void that was once filled with song,
imagination, narrative, drama, splashing water,
or the tiniest of coughs was now empty
just bright vacant walls,
imprints of furniture left on the carpet,

REMNANTS OF A LIFE ONCE LIVED.

I FOUND MYSELF DEAD TO THE WORLD.

THEY SAID TO SEEK OUT HAPPINESS
TO FIND DISTRACTION,
TO CARE FOR MYSELF, TO MOVE ONWARD,
TO REDEFINE ME,
BUT ONE CANNOT RETRIEVE HAPPINESS
OR FIND IT IN EMPTY MEADOWS,
THERE IS NO DISTRACTION FROM DEPRESSION,
IT IS ALL CONSUMING.
CARING FOR ONESELF, WITHOUT PURPOSE, IS AN ELIXIR
FOR BENIGN ILLNESS, TO MOVE ONWARD, WELL,
THERE'S NO CHOICE NOW IS THERE?

SO I SIT AND STARE FORWARD
AT THE HIGH DEFINITION FIGURES
IN FICTITIOUS OR BASED-ON-TRUE-EVENTS STORIES,
WISHING THAT I LED AN ENTIRELY DIFFERENT LIFE,
NOT REGRETTING A MOMENT IN PASSING,
BUT MY ENTIRE EXISTENCE.

TRANSLATION, GOD LISTENS: BITTER

I WOKE UP TO A CROWD OF ANXIOUS VOICES
WRINKLED FACES, WRINGING HANDS,
ASKING TOO MANY QUESTIONS,
SOMEWHERE AMONGST THEM,
I COULD HEAR MYSELF THINK INCANTATIONS
APPLY BEAUTY, SHE MUST REMEMBER YOU WERE PRETTY
FRAGRANCE, SHE MIGHT REMEMBER YOUR ESSENCE,
VIOLETS PRESSED AGAINST MY NECK.

THE CROWD STIRRED WITH MY EVERY RESTLESS MOVEMENT
FROM ROOM TO ROOM,
MATERIALS FLYING LIKE SILK SCARVES
IN A CHINESE ACROBAT CIRCUS ACT,
BE SOFT...

I COULD HEAR A WHISPER AMONG THEM,
WORDS, PASSING THROUGH THEM
LIKE OFFERING PLATES,
DEACONS WAITING AT EACH END OF THE CHURCH PEW,
DECEMBER TO DECEMBER,
WILL SHE REMEMBER?
ABANDONMENT. FORGOTTEN. INDIFFERENCE.

WAITING FOR REDEMPTION,
WITH LOVED ONES, UNDER HOSPITAL LIGHT,
IN UNCOMFORTABLE CHAIRS, SHIFTING WEIGHT
FROM SIDE TO SIDE, ELBOWS TIRED
FROM HOLDING UP MY HEAD,
I WAIT TO HEAR THE THE RESULTS

FROM THE TRAGEDY, CRITICAL CONDITION SURGERY,
EVERYTHING IS STERILE,
QUIET, LIKE A FIRST SNOW,
IT COMES OUT, REMOVES ITS MASK
TO BENEATH ITS CHILLED CHIN,
SNAPS OFF GLOVES AND ANSWERS...
SHE COMES RUNNING,
WRAPS HER ARMS AROUND ME, AND HOLDS ME.
(THE CROWD DISPERSES
TO BETTER THINGS TO DO.)

SHE SAYS,

YOU MUST HAVE BEEN FAR FAR AWAY
BECAUSE IT TOOK YOU A LONG TIME TO
GET HERE...

POETRY IS FOR MENTAL CASES, LOVEBIRDS AND THE DEAD

DIRTY NEEDLE
SCRATCHING
THE RECORD
PLAYER.

MOTEL OF CHOICE TONIGHT, OFF THE 405
LAYING UNDER STIFF SHEETS
BLAMING IT ON ME, VILIFIED AND DENIED.

IT'S THE WAY, SHRUG SHOULDERS, DEVELOP MENTAL DISORDERS
AND SMOKE MORE CIGARETTES, TASTING TIN-NY REGRET
ON THE TIP OF MY TONGUE THAT WANTS TO LASH OUT
AND GIVE IT TO YOU, BLOW DOWN YOUR HOUSE,
SUCK THAT EGO OUT OF YOUR THICK HEAD
AND BEAT YOUR HARD HEART INTO SENSE
BUT IT'S ALL MY FAULT.

SO I KICK THE WALL, REALIZE I'M NOT SO HURT,
BUT FEELING EMPTY IN A SEPIA HOLLOW WAY,
WELL IS RUNNING DRY AGAIN
AND NO ONE WANTS TO TREAD THIS TERRITORY ANYMORE,
EITHER TIME TO MOVE ON
OR SUCCUMB TO THE SITUATION AT HAND.

I'M TIRED
BUT I'M MORE TIRED OF LISTENING
TO EVERYTHING YOU THINK YOU KNOW ABOUT ME
MISSPOKEN WHILE YOU NEGLECT
EVERYTHING I'VE CLEARLY SAID.

AMUSEMENT PARK

YOU'RE LIKE A CIRCUS —
FULL OF COLOR, LAUGHTER
AMAZING ACTS
THAT LEAVE ONE BREATHLESS AFTER
YOU'RE LIKE A CARNIVAL —
FULL OF EXCITEMENT,
PRIZES OF SWEETHEART ROMANCE
DARING AND TEMPTING
WITH YOUR GAMES OF CHANCE
YOU'RE LIKE A MAGICIAN —
YOUR PERFORMANCE IS ALWAYS CAPTIVATING,
BUT WHEN YOUR SECRETS ARE TOLD —
THE DISAPPOINTMENT OF BEING LIED TO
RUINS THE TRADITION
THE CIRCUS ALWAYS RUNS AWAY,
THE CARNIVAL PACKS UP AND LEAVES,
A MAGICIAN ALWAYS DISAPPEARS
IT'S NO WONDER THERE'S NO AMUSEMENT,
WHEN YOU'RE NOT HERE

DUST DEVILS

The crew stole Aeolus' purse,
When it opened the winds took on terrestrial forms,
A paroxysm of storms called *Poets and Writers*—
Squalling self importance,
Filled with idle words propagating doubt
From spectators and admires alike
It was followed by gales of resentment,
Superiority to the land and sea
Made them free to wander aimlessly
And who dare question the way the wind blows?
A precipitation of pretentious entitlements,
Questioning the echo of the bow

Sulking in seething silence,
Vociferous derechos they were,
Clamoring importance,
Making the journey become prosaic,
Storm after storm,
Short days followed by long nights,
Sunburns, chapped lips and blisters
Then more,
More
On a scale that not even Beaufort could calculate

Their abrasive and self-serving manners
Eroding the delicate and beautiful nature
Of what lays before them,
Suspending everything worthwhile
In tumultuous chaos,
Leaving nothing but debris.

FUGUE

TELL ALL AND TELL NO ONE
THE BOOKENDS OF CONVERSATION

SHE SEES HIS EYES BEHIND THE MASK
TEARS MIMIC RAIN ON A WINDOW PANE,
HOLDING STILL AND TREMBLING AROUND THE IRIS
A PROMISE, A PRISM, A BLACKHOLE INTO THE UNDERWORLD
OF HIS SOUL, SHE SEES, THE AURA
IS AUDIBLE, THE AMPLITUDE IS DEAFENING
AND SHE REMAINS NEUTRALIZED
UNABLE TO SHIFT

IT WAS MY GIFT TO YOU, SHE SAYS.

HE KNOWS NO JOY, A PRELUDE
TO HER FUGUE, LOST WITHOUT
MEMORY, ALTRUISTIC THE EGO
BURIES ITS STICKS AND THE
OTHER BONES.

YOU ARE NOT ALONE, SHE MUTTERS.

TO DO LIST

FILE BANKRUPTCY
SEARCH FOR A MORE FULFILLING JOB,
GET MY HAIR DONE,
SHAVE MY LEGS
APPEAR HUMAN.
FEED THE CATS AGAIN

APPLY FOR MORE STUDENT LOANS
SO I CAN GET A DEGREE IN SOMETHING USEFUL
LIKE POETRY,
CREATIVE WRITING,
OR JOURNALISM
I WILL WRITE PROSE WITH FLARE AND SPEAK
THE TRUTH TO MASSES; AND THEY WILL LISTEN
TO MY ACCREDITED OPINION.

WATCH MY CREDIT REPORT ONLINE
BEFORE SOMEONE STEALS MY IDENTITY
AND GETS DECLINED,

PLAN THAT ULTIMATE VACATION TO A FOREIGN LAND
WHERE I WILL APPRECIATE ART FOR THE FIRST TIME,
SUDDENLY BECOME SPIRITUALLY ENLIGHTENED,
FILL THE POCKETS OF PEASANTS AND COME HOME
WITH FINE LEATHER GOODS AND RICH RED WINES
FOR THE AMPLE DINNER PARTIES I'LL THROW
WITH THE NUMEROUS FRIENDS
WHO ADORE MY COMPANY

LOSE THAT EXTRA WEIGHT THAT INFLATES MY CHEST,
BUBBLES MY STOMACH
AND BURDENS MY IDEAL DRESS SIZE
WITH STRETCH MATERIAL

MAKE THAT HEALTHY DINNER
AFTER A NICE WORK OUT AT THE GYM;
DIFFERENTIATING FROM THE LIGHT MEAL
AND CARDIO I DID THE DAY BEFORE,

YES.

QUIT SMOKING AND TAKE MY BIRTH CONTROL REGULARLY

STOP EATING PRESCRIPTION PILLS
LIKE BLUE AND PINK SWEET TARTS
GO TO CHURCH AND SING A HYMNAL,
GIVE TO CHARITY
WRITE LETTERS HOME ON ARGYLE STATIONERY
IN TEAL INK DECLARING
I FINALLY HAVE
PURPOSE.

ENCOUNTERS

FREE NIGHT, INSERT KEY.

ROUTINE GETS ICE,
POURS DRINKS WHILE SHE SEEKS COMFORT,
DRAWS HOT WATER, SINKS IN
AND RELAXES.

HER HANDS MAP HIS FRECKLED LANDSCAPE
WHILE RECOLLECTIONS OF PAST LIVES
AND REINCARNATED LOVE
BECOME INCANTATIONS OF THE FUTURE.

NAKED, EYES WIDE OPEN,
WATCHING IN LUSTFUL ADMIRATION,
CLIMAXING AND CLINGING ON FOR DEAR LIFE,
THEIR INTENSITY BRINKS
AND RELEASES.

WINE GLASSES EMPTY, MARTINIS GONE DRY,
THEY ARE INTOXICATED PULLING
TOGETHER THEIR SENSES, LIGHTERS AND CIGARETTES.

SMOKING IN FRONT OF GLASS DOORS,
FREE RIDE, THEY DEPART
ON A SHUTTLE TO THE AIRPORT,
TOO POOR TO TRAVEL
AND THE BAR WAS, OF COURSE, CLOSED
BACK TO THE TERMINAL
UNDER CONSTRUCTION, THEY DETOUR

TO A NEARBY HOTEL BAR
WHERE HE PURPOSELY WATCHES HER
FROM ACROSS THE ROOM
AS THE LONELY DRUNKEN SALES MEN
SHEEPISHLY-SMILE-WOLF-GRIN;
SHE ABANDONS ALL HOPE AND HER GLASS OF WINE.

THEY HOLD HANDS, SING SONG THROUGH
THE DARK NIGHT, CLIMBING IRON FENCES,
KNOCKING ON GLASS WINDOWS, ALL THE S/WAY
BACK TO THE ROOM, WHERE TIME IS LOST.

SPREAD WIDE OPEN, HE CLOSES THE CURTAINS AT 5 A.M.

TRAFFIC HAS RISEN, HAD COFFEE
AND BEEN THROUGH THE FAST FOOD DRIVE THROUGH,
AND IT IS NOW STALLED IN BETWEEN LANES ON-TIME
AND RUNNING LATE.

HIS FACE IS A LOST CHILD, THE BOND WAS FUSED
LAST NIGHT, RAW, WELDED TOGETHER, SOLDERED
JUST ENOUGH TO HAVE MERGED, UNBROKEN,
SILVER AND SHINING BEAUTIFULLY

SHE IS PUNISHED BY SLEEP DEPRIVATION
FOR RELISHING IN SELFISH DESIRE
INDESCRIBABLE PLEASURE, AGAIN,
AND AGAIN
SHE HAS GIVEN HIM
ALL
AND HE IS SO SAD TO WATCH
THE SHELL
OF HER LEAVE.

She pulls his face to her mouth,
kisses him
with all that is left.

The concrete, lights, signals —
all direct her way, while
he stays
just a little bit longer.

BIBLICAL APPROACH

THEY CAME RUNNING TO ME
LIKE I WAS THEIR MOTHER,
LIKE I HAD FOOD, OR WATER
AND THEY WERE THIRSTY.

THEY TOLD ME ANYTHING
I NEEDED TO HEAR
LIKE THEY WERE JUNKIES,
I WAS THE BANK OR MAYBE JESUS
WHEN THEY WERE MOMENTARILY SORRY.

I WAS ALMOST NAKED WHEN THEY LEFT.

I WAS NEARLY STARVED

UNTIL THEY CAME BACK.

GOOD YEAR

IN THE SKY AT THIRTY-FIVE MILES PER HOUR,
PRIOR TO OUR EXIT, THE INCIDENT REPORT
HAD BEEN FAIRLY CASUAL, LESS ONE GERMAN PILOT,
WHO WAS BURNED ALIVE,
HIS ENTIRE PASSENGER LIST JUMPING OFF THE SIDE,
WALKING AWAY FINE,
WHILE THIRTY-FIVE SLOW ON-LOOKERS
WERE CAUGHT IN THE FLAMES
OF THE SHREDDED MATERIALS
IN THE FIELD.

THE VELOCITY AT WHICH SHE PUSHED ME
REACHED THE SEARS TOWER, AND THE STRENGTH
IN WHICH I PULLED HER DOWN
WAS THE HEAVIEST PULL UP I'D EVER DONE,
ONLY TO FALL.

FREE FALLING TO DEATH AT *120* MILES PER HOUR,
WHILE THE GOODYEAR BLIMP STRODE BY
MURKILY HUMMING AT LESS THAN A VISIBLE PACE,
CRASHING INTO EARTH,
CHEEKS SMASHED INTO THE GRASS,
JUST LIKE THE TIME I FELL OFF THE BICYCLE HANDLE BARS
AND SHE LET ME LAY UNCONSCIOUS, WATCHING TV
TELLING DAD SHE DIDN'T KNOW WHERE I WAS,
WAKING UP JUST IN TIME TO HAVE HIM GRAB ME UP
FROM THE GROUND, ELBOW IN FIST,
OTHER HAND SMACKING MY LEG,
WHILE SHE SMIRKED, QUIETLY.

NO ONE CARED WHO
STARTED IT.

SHE'S A GONER,
TERMINALLY ILL.
I AM BLEEDING FROM THE LIPS,
I AM SMASHED UP TO BITS.

TRYING,
TO REACH FOR HER HAND,
JUST IN CASE,
THERE'S A PULSE.

PORTAMENTI

IT BEGINS
BREATH ON NECK,
HANDS ARRANGING
HER
EVER SO SLIGHTLY,
BENDING RESTRAINT
AND WILLING
HER TO GIVE—
A SOFT MOAN,
WHISPERING GENTLY,
REASSURING IN THE DARKNESS,
RENDERING THE ROOM
TO MOVEMENT, RHYTHM,
A MONTAGE OF ECSTASY GIVING
A EUPHONY OF SOUND IN TANDEM,
SHE'S BECOME
A TREMBLING TIMBRE
TO HIS INSTRUMENTAL ABILITIES—
RESONANT.
A SENSE OF GLISSANDO
ARTICULATING THROUGH
CRETIC CLIMAXING, INFINITIVE
GERUNDS TO PLEASURE,
IT IS WITHOUT
MEASURE NOR LYRIC
THAT THEY ENVELOPE
ONE ANOTHER, CADENCED
BY HEARTBEAT...
THEY DRIFT TO SLEEP

CONSOLATION DOUBLE

SOMEONE TOOK MY FLAG
OUT OF THE MOON
THERE'S NO EVIDENCE I
WAS EVER HERE
FIRST, WORSE,
I WAS ASKED TO LEAVE!
DON'T WORRY, I'LL LOCK THE DOOR
BEHIND ME.

SOMEONE SIGN THE TREATY—
PLEASE LOUISE, NO ANNA!
JUST MAKE A PURCHASE
AND DEFINE TERRITORY
MARKINGS LATER WITH THE
CAT MEWLING IN THE KITCHEN
AS MY HIGH PITCH
GETS DEFINITION CALLING
OUT TO HER, AS IF,
TO SAY I'M HERE,
IT'S OKAY.

CASH HERE, ACROSS THE BOARD
I LAUGH, THREE THE HARD WAY,
SCRATCHED, LEAVING ALSO ELIGIBLE
HOPE FROM ATROPHY, THE DISTAFF RACE,
WHERE NO ONE
CAN EVER WIN,

EASED INTO SECOND
PLACE, AGAIN.

PERTAINYMS

WORDS DRIBBLING OUT LIKE THE SALIVA OF A MANIAC'S MOUTH,
BREATH LIKE WET NEWSPAPER INK
AND STENCH OF THE LOCAL NEWS, SPITTING
THE WEATHER REPORT TO THE PAVEMENT IN THE RAIN.

YOU'RE IN THE DARK AND YOU'RE AFRAID.
YOU'RE IN THE BAG
AND THE BOTTLES OVER YOUR HEAD.
CUT ACROSS THE STREET, DASH UP THE CURB
TO THE SIDEWALK, WISH YOU WERE DEAD
AND THREATEN THE OPEN WINDOWS,
FLOWERS POTS FALLING, PROMISES,
PROMISES

OUT OF BREATH ARGUMENTS STOP,
BENT OVER, HANDS ON KNEES,
WHY WON'T YOU LISTEN TO ME,
JUST ONCE PLEASE? A VOICE SCREAMS IN THE WIND
AND I THOUGHT I HEARD YOU SINGING AGAIN,
IT WASN'T OUR SONG
AND THE STATION GOT LOST IN THE TURN
OF THE DIAL WHILE
SCRATCHING SPARSE WORDS AND SCARCE
SOUNDS THROUGH THE SPEAKER.

YOU WERE ALWAYS SO CHARMING,
YOU WERE THE ONE AND ONLY
AND WILL ALWAYS BE, SHE THINKS AND HE DRIFTS
INTO OPOSSUM SLEEP.

I'M SORRY, I HAVE TO GO NOW,
SHUFFLING TO THE DOOR,
SHE'S GOING TO MOVE BACK TO KANSAS CITY.

HE STRIKES GOLD, BRINGS HOME HIS EMPTY CUP,
OFFERS HER APOLOGIES LIKE SIMULATED GEM STONES,
ALMOST TOO GOOD TO BE TRUE,
AND FORGETS EVERYTHING ELSE THAT WAS SAID
AND SHE BECOMES OF AGE, COLD AND DISTANT IN THE HEAT
OF THE MOMENT
HE FINDS THE LAST OF HER WARMTH;
LEAVES HER NAKED, LYING ON THE BED
BENEATH THE COOL OF THE FAN,
SWEAT BEADS LIKE HIPPIE DAISY CHAINS
AND THE LAST
SCENT OF SUMMER FLOWERS
AFTER A HUMID RAIN.

TAXING THE TARMAC

SHE SAID
PLEASE DON'T BACK INTO ME.
EVERYTHING LOOKED LIKE REVERSE LIGHTS.
EVERYTHING GLOWED LIKE CHRISTMAS.
PLEASE PLEASE PLEASE

THE BURN MARKS WERE BACK
LIKE TIRES VEERING OFF THE ROAD,
TOO LATE TO ESCAPE CERTAIN DEATH

SHE WAS SAYING PLEASE
DISTRACTED BY

DON'T - BACK - INTO - ME PARANOIA.

RED AND WHITE ALL IN FRONT OF HER;
OBSCURE AND BLURRED.
THE WATER TASTED TONIC.
CITRUS WAS TOXIC ON HER TONGUE
AND CAFFEINE ACHED HER ROT
STOMACH UP IN KNOTS.
SITTING ALONE, LISTENING TO THE RADIO
IN THE RITE AID PARKING LOT.

COME HERE, WHAT DID YOU SAY?

Wayside,
left behind, in an alley,
empty in a brown bag,
discarded with only shameful
remnants on your breath
easily disguised by your cigarette.

Standing in front of an elementary school, waiting,
a little boy runs to his first crush,
embraces the memory
and stares long after the sunset
from his second floor apartment.

The picture of her through his cracked lens
eventually disappears from broken sight.

Silence filled with another,
he apologizes.

The next day comes into focus,
void of sun, heat, or promise.
She waits. He doesn't speak
much, if at all.

It was the last time, this time,
it was the last. She parks the car
underneath the carport, pulls the emergency brake,
hands on the wheel she shudders
and weeps.

THE BEST REVENGE ON A LIAR IS TO CONVINCE THEM YOU BELIEVE

I PAUSED AND ADMIRED THE WELL MANICURED
LAWNS OF YOUR LIES, THE TRIMMED AND CREATIVE
FOLIAGE FENCES YOU PLACED BETWEEN YOU AND ME.

I STARED AT THE HOME WE BUILT,
IT WAS FILLED WITH LIGHT,
WAITING UP LATE,
THE SAME HOME WE GAVE WARMTH,
THROUGH SWEAT DRIVEN LUST AND
CANDLED SHADOWS ON THE WALL
LISTENING TO OLD TIME RADIO SHOWS
SCRATCHING OVER THE SPEAKER, WHILE WE LAID IN BED, NAKED.

THE RESIDENCE OF OUR FUTURE SELVES,
WHERE WE FILLED THE WALLS WITH CONFESSIONS.

THE SIGNED, READY TO PAY THE PRICE, CONTRACT
BOUND RESPONSIBILITY WE WOULD PILLAR INTO
A LIFETIME OF MEMORIES, THE PLACE WHERE WE BOUGHT IN
AND WENT FROM BASIC TO THE UPGRADED,
STOP AT ANY MOMENT AND REWIND IT BACK,
CABLE PACKAGE OF OUR DREAMS,
WHERE YOU WERE, FOR SOME MERE ADDITIONAL CHANGE,
WIRELESSLY CONNECTED TO THE OUTSIDE,
A WORLD OF NO OBLIGATIONS, NO STRINGS
ATTACHED PUPPETRY, AN UNDERGROUND CATACOMB
OF CASUAL CONVERSATION, ENCOUNTERS AND GAMES OF CHANCE,
CHATTING IT UP WITH POKER BUDDIES,
A NEIGHBORHOOD IN WHICH YOU WERE OFTEN FOUND

HELPING AUTISM-AFFLICTED MOTHERS PICK PRODUCE,
FRESHER, BETTER THAN WHAT WAITED FOR THEM AT HOME,
YOU WERE SEAMLESSLY SKY PEEING ACROSS THE CLOUDS,
WRITING YOUR NAME LIKE A DUSTER AIRPLANE PROPOSING
THE UNTHINKABLE AND LISTENING TO THEM GIGGLE
ON THE PHONE LINE, YOU WERE PROMISING RAIN
LIKE A TRAVELING VAUDEVILLIAN DOCTOR,
SERUMS AND CURES, BAITING WITH PROMISES,
SATISFACTION, SYCOPHANT REFERENCES
(ALL AS COLORFUL LURES) AND I WAS REELED IN,
NOT BY THE MOCK CONFIDENCE OR YOUR DOMINATE APPROACH,
I WAS SOLD BY YOU
NOT BECAUSE, YOU, WOULD MAKE ME WELL,
BUT, BY THE APOLOGY, THE BACK PEDAL OF YOUR SECURITY,
THE GENTLEMEN BENEATH THE BRAVADO
WHO WANTED ME A LITTLE TOO MUCH BUT
NEEDED ME JUST ENOUGH TO BE BETTER THAN THE CONCOCTIONS
HE BOTTLED UP AND SHELVED INSIDE THAT TRAILER HE PACKED UP
AND DRAGGED TO THE NEXT TOWN WITH THE STEALTH ABILITY
LIKE THAT OF A CARNIE TEARING DOWN THE RIDES
AT THE HOUR OF THE WOLF, JUST ON THE OUTSKIRTS OF TOWN
BEFORE DAWN, BEFORE ANYONE NOTICED,
ANYTHING, OR ANYONE
WAS GONE.
I WASN'T JUST CURED IN
THE FORE-HEAD-SLAP EVANGELISTIC, I'VE CUM TO JESUS,
SEEN GOD AND CAN SPREAD
THE WORD WAY —
I WAS HIS CURE
HIS FIX,
HIS

AND THAT CURED ME,
LIKE PICKLED FEET IN BRINE.

GUILT RIDDEN (BET ON THAT HORSE). ENCORE AT HOLLYWOOD PARK. (EXACTA BOX)

WHEN WAS IT THAT YOU FINALLY FELT GUILT
FOR STEPPING OUT, ON ME,
I CAN SEE YOU NOW,
SHAKING MY DOORMAT DUST OFF
THE PORCH, CLEANING IT UP FOR NO ONE TO SEE,
I FEEL YOUR FEET FIRMLY PLANTED, SCRAPING
OFF THE SHIT YOU DRAGGED IN FROM THE NIGHT
BEFORE UNTIL THE MOMENT
WHEN YOU FINALLY LOOKED DOWN.

YOU SAW THE BRILLIANCE BEGIN TO FADE,
THAT I WAS GETTING WORN FOR THE WEAR
IT WAS AROUND THE TIME YOU STOPPED
BEING ANGRY FOR THE TIMES
YOU WERE SO SURE YOU NEEDED ME
AND I WASN'T THERE,
OR WAS IT WHEN YOU FINALLY REALIZED
THE ONLY ONE CHEATING, WAS INDEED, YOU,
MAYBE IT WAS THAT DAY IN THE KITCHEN,
YOU SAW IT IN MY EYES, WHEN I DESCRIBED
YOUR INDISCRETIONS TO YOU IN PERFECT PEACE,
IT COULDN'T HAVE BEEN WHEN I BEGGED YOU
TO STOP AND TO LOVE ME.

OR WAS IT
THE POINT OF NO RETURN, THAT FAMILIAR BLOCK,
WHERE I STOPPED ASKING YOU
THE W'S.

EMERGENCE. SEE.
(WHAT YOU MADE ME DO BEHAVIOR)

OFF KILTER, OUT OF SORTS
FULL OF WOE-IS-ME-ACCOUNTABILITY
AND ACCUSATIONS AGAINST THE WORLD,
MOSTLY HER THOUGH.
SHE IS LISTENING, BARELY DRINKING.
SHE'S NO FUN TONIGHT, MAN, NO FUN.
LIKE JAZZ THAT'S TOO SLOW GOING,
LIKE NOT VIBING, LIKE SHE ISN'T KEEPING
WITH THE RHYTHM, MAN, SHE LET'S GO OF HAND,
GIVES UP AGITATED, SHE CAN'T DANCE,
BUT WHERE IS SHE GOING?

SHE'S SLEEPING,
DREAMING, YOU'RE KEEPING TIME WITH THE DEVIL
AND CRAWLING AMONG THE DESPERATE
DESIRES THAT ARE LEFT ON THE DANCE FLOOR
AT ONE-FIFTY-NINE AM SWINGING CHANDELIERS,
DOORS, COUPLES OPEN TO A THIRD PARTY
LONELY, UGLY AND WILLING
THE FAT GIRLS STAND OUTSIDE,
LAUGHING, MAKING DRUNK ANNOUNCEMENTS
LIKE NEON SIGNAGE AT THE CASH ADVANCE SHOP ON THE CORNER,
OR CLOSETED AND SCARED, BEHIND, BENEATH,
BETWEEN A SHEET, YOU DIAL IN LIKE THE VICTIM
TO NINE-ONE-ONE.

MUTATIONS

POKE THE TADPOLES WITH A STICK,
TERROR ON THE RIVER, JUVENILE EXPLORATION,
BAREFOOT IN MUD, THE SURE FOOT SLIDES,
WHILE THE HANDS STABILIZE
A POTENTIAL FALL
HOLDING ONTO THE TRUNK OF THE OAK TREE.
DON'T YOU DARE LEAVE, FALL
OFF
THIS WEAKENING BRANCH, OR BREAK
FREE.

CREAM THE COFFEE, STIR IT IN,
TWIZZLE STICK, THE PERFECT FIT,
INSTANT TO PERCOLATING, THE WATER GETS HOT, BURNS,
AND ALL TOO SOON EVAPORATES.

OPEN THE UMBRELLA TO AVOID THE CASCADE
OF RAIN STRINGING DOWN LIKE BLUEGRASS SONGS OFF A GUITAR,
YOU KNEW WHEN YOU LEFT IT WAS INEVITABLE
THAT YOU WOULD GET WET, IN FACT, DRENCHED
IN THE SHAME OF YOUR GUILTY SWEAT,
DON'T SAY YOU DIDN'T,
YOU KNEW JUST ENOUGH TO BRING YOUR UMBRELLA,
YOU WERE SWINGING THE HANDLE DOWN THE STREET,
WHILE THE CLOUDS HAD CAUCUS
AND THE STORM BEGAN TO BREW;
DON'T SAY YOU DIDN'T,
WHEN CLEARLY,
YOU DAMN WELL KNEW.

LACK LUST HERE

HIS DARKNESS BROODS NAVY
SHINING IN THE CORNER OF THE ROOM
HER HEART BEATS,
I EXIST, I EXIST,
I EXIST
EMPTY

EXHALE CARCINOGENIC
ASH, DULL GRAY, DIRTY SPECKS,
SCRATCHING AT HER FACE,
NERVOUS MOVEMENTS,
HE THINKS SHE'S NOT COPING,
IS UNRAVELING, AND NOT WORTH
SAVING,

(SUDDEN JERKS SHE THINKS)

UNDER BREATH, HE READS LIPS,
BREAKS THE TIP
OF THE PENCIL
AND SHE WRITES ON AND ON,
WHILE HE WATCHES THE LACE OF HER
SCRIPT TELL ALL, POST

SHE ACHES IN PAINS
SHE CANCELS AGAIN, SHE SITS ALONE
MODERN COMMUNICATION FAILS HER
SHE IS INVISIBLE NOW
TO THEM ALL.

SHE CRIES IN THE BATH EVERY NIGHT,
NINE NEAR THE DOT,
HER TEARS SEPARATING THE FOAM
FROM LUKEWARM WATER,
DISSIPATING QUICKLY LIKE FIRE TO FLASH PAPER,
NO MAGIC HERE,
NAKED, ALONE, CLEAN AND BARE,
NO ONE TO TOUCH HER,
NO ONE LEFT THAT CARES, NO ONE CALLING,
WRITING, THINKING OF HER NAME,
THEY HAVE SOMEWHERE ELSE TO GO,
SOMEONE ELSE ON THEIR MINDS,
A DIFFERENT PAIR OF SHOES,
A NEW LOOK, ABLE TO CLICK HEELS ON THE SIDEWALK,
PUSH DOORS OPEN SWINGING WIDE,
GRAND CHAMPAGNE ENTRANCES,
TOSSING SCARVES ON HOOKS,
REMOVING WINTER COATS AND CREATING HEARTH,
WITH SOMEONE YOUNGER, PRETTIER,
DIFFERENT, IT SEEMS
OLD FLAMES, WITHER, LACK LUSTER,
TALK TOO MUCH ABOUT THE PAST
AND AGE,

NOTHING'S MORE EXCITING
THAN THE PROSPECT OF MAYBE,

AND THERE SHE IS
SIPPING AIR LIKE SHE CAN BARELY
STAND THE TASTE OF IT
HARDLY VISIBLE IN THE SIXTY-WATT
SOFT WHITE LIGHT PUSHING HALF CIRCLES
ON THE WALL,

SHE IS THINKING LONELY, LEAVES HER ROOM
FOR A MEDIOCRE ATTEMPT TO BELONG
IN A ROOM FULL OF INTERACTION,
FEELING UTTERLY DEPRESSED,
AND DOWN RIGHT UNCOMFORTABLE
IN HER OWN HOME AND SKIN,
IT'S NO WONDER,
SHE'S SCRATCHING HERSELF THIN,
WANDERING FROM ROOM TO ROOM,
SMOKING CIGARETTE AFTER CIGARETTE,
WHY, IT'S SIMPLE REALLY,
HER EXISTENCE,
HAS BECOME
QUITE PATHETIC,
EVEN TO HER
MOROSE SHRINKING SENSE
OF SELF.

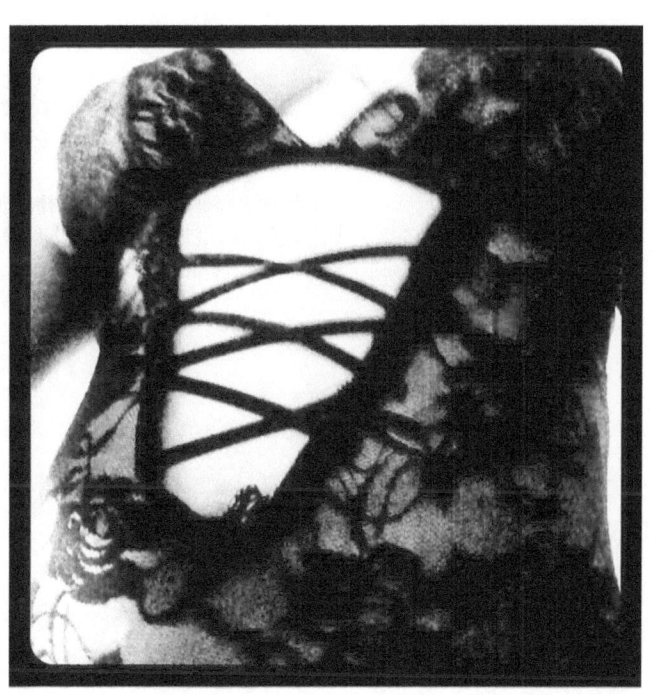

FRAGMENTS

SOLITAIRE

HE WAS PLAYING RECORDS
SHE WAS TOSSING ACES
NEITHER ONE AWARE
THEY WERE LOSING AT THE GAME

HIS HAIR WAS GETTING THINNER
THE WALLS WERE GROWING BARE
NEITHER SCRATCHED THE SURFACE
OR SEEMED TO NOTICE
THE OTHER ONE
EXISTED.

(AND SOMEWHERE, VULTURES CIRCLED IN FOR LANDING)

LOST IN TRANSLATION

CARBON DIDN'T COPY
SO TYPE LOST ITS FACE
MINUTES TO THE WHISTLE
WET HAD LOST HER TASTE
SHE BLEW BETWEEN LIPS
BUT IT ALL CAME OUT CRACKERS,
SALTY
DRY

AND ALL OVER
THE PLACE.

MATH SKILLS

WITH NOTHING LEFT IN COMMON
THE DENOMINATOR
DIVIDES
----------------SPLITS
AND RUNS INTO THE NEXT
LOWEST LEVEL OF ITS SPECIES.

SOMEI YOSHINO - MONO NO AWARE

THE CHERRY BLOSSOM PETALS FALL
LIKE SNOW, PASSING OVER THE GROUND
DRIFTING LIKE CLOUDS,
PLEASURE REINCARNATED, TINGED TO THE STEM
IN THE PALEST OF PINKS, A DREAM SPREADING
ACROSS THE FLOOR, ENTANGLED, SURRENDERING
TO CONQUER, THE BLOSSOM QUIVERS,
TREMBLES LOOSELY, EPHEMERAL

THE WIND CARRIES YAKIKO YOSANO'S
POETRY IN A WHISPER THROUGH THE BRANCHES,
FINGERS INTERTWINED, PRESSING FLOWERS
INTO PERFUME

WISTFULLY AWARE
OF IMPERMANENCE
ALL THINGS POSSIBLE
MUFFLED IN MOAN, NESTLED
IN AN EMBRACE

THREE MARKS OF EXISTENCE
LOST FOR THE MOMENT, IN FLUX,
IN LOSS, IN BIRTH AND EMPTINESS
IN SELF, THE ROOTS THIRST
FOR MORE WATER, THE TRUNK SWALLOWS
SELFISHLY AND SHAKES THE LEAVES
UNTIL THE FLOWERS FALL AGAIN

ARS LONGA, VITA BREVIS

You watch my lips move
(not a word to say)
Everything is for you;
I push you back,
And linger linear until
The reciprocal nature of you,
Divides me and I am fading
Into half between the candles flickering illumination
Through 1948 star-engraved Escher skies;
Chet Baker is carrying the weight of sound
As a backdrop to our shadows,
Glancing at our reflection,
A silver screen;
I succumb to the strength of your hands;
And the silk of your flesh,
We are fashionably naked,
And considerably underdressed;
Colliding until we exhaust ambition,
Lure ourselves outside,
Catch our breath,
Lose minutes to attention deficit while I think

I've got your number

While you were talking
I was listening priori,
And I don't need to know,
Just come closer and walk awhile with me,
Just be, primrose,

BEFORE THE PATH
GETS LIBERTINE STEEP
AND THORN BLOWN BY THE CARELESS WINDS
ON THE WAY TO HEAVEN;

I WANT TO FALL ASLEEP IN THIS PREMISE
BEFORE THE MOON RELINQUISHES,
ANTECEDENT TO THE DAWN,
BEFORE ALL RETURNS TO PLACE AS IF WITHOUT
TRACE AND I AM NO LONGER DREAMING,
FORCED AWAKE
IN THE EVIDENCE OF ABSENCE.

TRAIL HER TRASH

She was one to get around the park,
mid-day she was hung out to dry on the clothesline,
come night, she was a tube-top tigress
stealthily seeking her prey,
disability checks in?
social security deposited?
cash it, drink it,
smoke it, spit it out, scope it out
and move onto the next
mark.

She never managed
to travel too much past the backyard
of her trailer;

A life full of tin can promises,
day dreaming on metal step porches
that never touched the astroturf
the asphalt walk ways were the comforts
of what she considered home,
just off the highway,
beyond the dirt road and bramble
of Independence Road.

She was not known for much more
than her presence, absolutely diseased,
her pieces
of pie had been sliced a part

AND SPREAD ACROSS ALMOST ALL THE PICNIC TABLES,
FROM JUNIPER COURT
TO HOLLOWAY LANE, SOMETIMES EVEN
ON THE MOUND ON ANGEL HEIGHTS,
CATCH HER STANCE, SQUAT DOWN BEFORE KNEELING,

SHE WAS KNOWN
FOR HER INABILITY TO STOP THE PLAYERS
FROM STEALING BASES,
JUST SHY OF TWENTY
SHE HAD THREE CHILDREN, EACH WITH A DIFFERENT RELATIVE
WHO DIDN'T KNOW MUCH BETTER,
THAN HER, ALL OF WHICH HAD OZARK MENTALITY
AND ARKANSAS CLASS.

SHE NEVER REALLY HAD MUCH OF A CHOICE,
LIVING OFF OF THE EXTENSION CORD TRAILING FROM
THE GENERATOR OF ANOTHER UNSUSPECTING NEIGHBOR.

Dear Laura

thank you for the nice
letter, I am fine, nice
you are too.

I just started the 2nd
grade. I canoot Leave now but
I mis you, I hope to see you soon.
I will give your Letter to my mom
to see what she says

from: sammie

ps I can't
read cursive. let
plese print

www.ingramcontent.com/pod-product-compliance
Lightning Source LLC
Chambersburg PA
CBHW030454010526
44118CB00011B/929